THUNDERSTORMS

BILL McAULIFFE

SCIENCE OF THE SKIES

Published by Creative Education
P.O. Box 227, Mankato, Minnesota 56002
Creative Education is an imprint of The Creative Company
www.thecreativecompany.us

Design and production by Liddy Walseth
Art direction by Rita Marshall
Printed by Corporate Graphics in the United States of America

Photographs by Alamy (Imagebroker, Andrea Matone), Corbis (Joe Bator,
Bettmann, Warren Faidley, Jon Hicks, Lewis Kemper/Monsoon Photolibrary, Jim
Reed, Jim Reed/Jim Reed Photography, TH-Foto), Dreamstime (Patty Jenks, Luca
Manieri, Marekuliasz, Demydenko Myhailo, Chris White), Getty Images (Grant
Faint, Image Source, Erik Simonsen, Don Smith, Jon Van de Grift/Visuals Unlimited,
Inc.), iStockphoto (Chieh Cheng, Steve Geer, Jane Norton, Yahor Piaskouski,
Charles Schug, Cindy Singleton, Clint Spencer, Vitaly Titov, Nick Tzolov)

Library of Congress Cataloging-in-Publication Data
McAuliffe, Bill.
Thunderstorms / by Bill McAuliffe.
p. cm. — (Science of the skies)
Summary: An exploration of thunderstorms, including how these warm-weather storms
develop, the phenomena of lightning and thunder, and how severe thunderstorms have
impacted human history.
Includes bibliographical references and index.
ISBN 978-1-58341-930-4
1. Thunderstorms—Juvenile literature. I. Title.

QC968.2.M43 2010
551.55'4—dc22 2009023526

CPSIA: 120109 PO1095

First Edition
2 4 6 8 9 7 5 3 1

CREATIVE C EDUCATION

THUNDERSTORMS

BILL McAULIFFE

SCIENCE OF THE SKIES

IT'S ANOTHER SUMMER DAY AT THE BEACH. AS THE SUN SOARS ACROSS THE SKY, PARENTS LATHER UP THEIR KIDS WITH SUNSCREEN, SUNBATHERS BAKE ON BLANKETS, AND THE CONCESSION STAND IS SELLING A LOT OF LEMONADE. BUT SUDDENLY A SHADOW SNEAKS ACROSS THE HOT SAND; THE SUN IS MASKED BY A HEAVY CLOUD CURTAIN. THERE'S A FLASH OF LIGHTNING, THEN A LOUD, LOW RUMBLE. THE LIFEGUARDS ORDER EVERYONE OUT OF THE WATER, AND SOON LIGHTNING FLASHES OVER THE BEACH, EAR-SPLITTING THUNDER CRACKS AND ROLLS, AND A DOWNPOUR HITS THE SAND. THUNDERSTORMS CAN BRING DESTRUCTIVE WINDS, HAMMERING HAIL, AND EVEN TORNADOES. BUT THIS TIME, IT'S OVER IN HALF AN HOUR. NO HARM'S BEEN DONE EXCEPT FOR A FEW SOAKED BEACH TOWELS. SOON THE SUN BREAKS THROUGH THE CLOUDS AGAIN, AND KIDS DASH BACK TO THE WATER. IT'S BEEN JUST ANOTHER THUNDERSTORM, ONE OF THE THRILLS OF A SUMMER AFTERNOON.

THE RECIPE FOR A STORM

It takes the sun to make a thunderstorm. But like a mischief-maker, the sun is usually long gone by the time the trouble starts. When sunlight penetrates Earth's atmosphere, it strikes the ground and heats it. This warmth, in turn, heats the air just above the ground. And because warm air is lighter than cold, heat always rises. This is one of the driving principles behind all weather, and one of the reasons why thunderstorms are a feature of warm weather but are rare in winter.

As warm air rises, it carries water vapor with it. This process is illustrated when water gets sprayed on hot pavement: the water will turn to visible rising steam and then **evaporate**. As the warmth lifts the vapor, though, it hits cooler air above. At about 3,000 feet (900 m), the cooling water vapor will **condense** into tiny droplets of water, making a visible white **cumulus** cloud. That innocent, cottony puff may be the beginning of a mighty thundercloud.

As the vapor condenses, it releases heat. This can cause the cloud to continue to rise and pull more warm air and water vapor into it, in what's known as the developing stage of a thundercloud. The cloud may continue to billow and rise ever skyward to altitudes of six to eight miles (10–13 km), where the surrounding air is so cold that the water droplets freeze and form hail and snow. The hail, taking on layer after layer of ice, might get heavy enough to begin falling through the updraft. It could melt into rain on the way down, adding to the heavy downpour from the cloud, or rattle the ground. At this point, the cumulus cloud is known as a cumulonimbus, meaning it's in its mature stage as a full-blown thunderstorm cloud.

In some cases, warm air rises forcefully enough (in a **supercell**, it can rise at 150 miles [240 km] per hour or more) that it finally bumps up against an atmospheric ceiling. Extremely cold, high-altitude winds might blow the top of the cloud off in one direction, creating the classic **anvil** shape of a mighty summer thundercloud. Or the cloud might spread out against the border of the **stratosphere**, about 10 miles (16 km) up, where temperatures of about –60 °F (–51 °C) block its rise, giving it a broader anvil shape.

Heat is a key element of the strongest thunderstorms—first in the high temperatures that evaporate moisture, and, often, then in the electricity a storm cloud can throw down.

WHERE'S THAT LIGHTNING?

*After the first **supersonic** crack, thunder travels "only" at the speed of sound, which is about one mile (1.6 km) every five seconds. Knowing that, it's easy to calculate the distance from the flash of lightning that made the thunder. Count the seconds between the flash and the sound of thunder, then divide the total by five. If it takes five seconds for the thunder to reach you, the lightning is one mile (1.6 km) away. The sound of thunder travels only about 15 miles (24 km). But lightning is visible for hundreds of miles on summer nights, as flashes called "heat lightning."*

Clouds with this top-heavy appearance are actually past their prime as thunderclouds and are considered to be in the **dissipating** stage. By this time, their frozen and liquid droplets have been falling through the updraft, cooling it and causing the updraft to weaken. If the cooling downdraft becomes stronger than the warm updraft, this cool air might sink to the ground and splash outward. While this effectively cuts off the large cloud's source of heat energy, it can kick up surrounding warm air, often giving birth to new thunderstorm cells.

Rain, hail, winds, and sometimes tornadoes are all produced by thunderstorms. But it takes thunder to make a thunderstorm. And it takes lightning to make thunder. Both are also manufactured by the thundercloud itself.

Frozen pellets of precipitation officially are called hail when they reach a width of at least 1/5 of an inch (5 mm); rain often takes on a noticeably whiter color just before hail arrives.

Lightning is a **current** of electricity not much wider than a finger that forms in an instant, with a temperature of about 55,000 °F (30,500 °C)—about five times hotter than the surface of the sun. That blast of heat can create a shock wave of rapidly expanding air, essentially a sonic boom, which we know as thunder. And because sound moves much more slowly than light, we always see lightning before we hear the thunder it makes.

The Navajo Indians of the southwestern United States believed thunder was caused when the Thunderbird, a storm god, flapped its wings. The Navajo welcomed the rain but feared the storms the Thunderbird brought. Even today there are many people who fear thunder. This condition is called brontophobia, derived from the Greek words for thunder (*brontē*) and fear (*phobos*). Pets and livestock often get anxious as much as an hour before humans even hear thunder. Some researchers believe the animals may be reacting to **infrasonic** sound waves from the coming storm.

People who study thunder have names for the different sounds thunder can make. Claps are sudden, loud sounds lasting 0.2 to 2 seconds. Peals are sounds that change in pitch, rolls are irregular and varying in sound, and rumbles are long-lasting, low-pitch sounds. Thunder that is produced nearby has been described

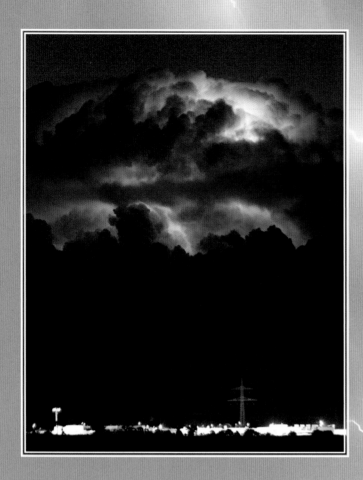

Although lightning can be both scary and deadly, it is undeniably spectacular, whether it occurs within vast cumulonimbus clouds (above) or as forked bolts (opposite).

as having a clicking or cloth-tearing sound, followed by something like a cannon shot or loud crack, then continuous rumbling.

Thunder is typically deflected upward from where it originates, because sound travels faster through cooler air, which is usually above the ground. It can also be made louder or softer by humidity, winds, clouds, and the landscape over which it travels. A nearby clap of thunder typically registers about 120 **decibels** (dB), a measure of sound that is 10 times louder than a jackhammer. Thunder that is very close can cause temporary deafness or permanent ear damage, but it's usually not as risky as some human activities, such as sitting in front of speakers at a rock concert, where the sound can be as loud as thunder for several hours straight. The quickly passing wave of air pressure from thunder has also been known to pop nails out of walls and break windows.

Distant, rumbling thunder can sometimes be mistaken for traffic, construction noise, or fireworks. Canoeists in wilderness areas have been known to mistake it for the sound of someone banging a paddle against an

aluminum canoe. The pitch of thunder changes as the sound waves are absorbed by surroundings, but the rumbling is due to the fact that the waves are emitted by different locations along the lengthy lightning bolts, thereby putting the sounds at different distances from the ear of the listener. Whatever it sounds like, thunder is an indication that lighting is near—and a reliable warning that it's time to head for cover.

The location of lightning determines how loud the thunder will be; lightning over empty ground (right) will likely be louder than that within cloud swells (below).

THE WATER CYCLE

*Thunderstorms are the engines that circulate Earth's water. When they drop rain, some soaks into the soil. Some sinks further into deep **aquifers**. About 80 percent falls on oceans. Water on the surface of land or the oceans evaporates into the atmosphere, and plants release vapor in a process called evapotranspiration. When this vapor rises and cools, it condenses into clouds, then into rain and other precipitation, and falls all over again. A molecule of water remains in the air an average of nine days before moving on in the cycle. But it can stay in the ocean, where it's less likely to change form, for thousands of years.*

UPDRAFTS, DOWNDRAFTS, & BLOWDOWNS

It's estimated that there are 2,000 thunderstorms happening on Earth at any moment, and 100,000 occur per year in the U.S. alone. Most bring welcome rain to crops and replenish water supplies. But some carry surprising and sometimes terrifying combinations of wind, rain, hail, and tornadoes.

There are several different types of thunderstorms. The most basic is the single-cell thunderstorm, a short-lived event lasting about half an hour. The single-cell storm has one updraft and one downdraft. Occasionally, a single-cell thunderstorm will meet the standard of a severe storm, which means it peppers the ground with hail at least three-quarters of an inch (1.9 cm) in **diameter**—about the size of a nickel—and develops winds of at least 58 miles (93 km) per hour.

The most common type of thunderstorm is the multi-cell cluster, made up of several single-cell storms moving as a group. Each cell might be in a different phase of thunderstorm development, with mature cells in the middle, dissipating cells on the leading edge, and new cells popping up on the trailing side. Each cell might live only about 20 minutes, but for people on the ground, the entire experience can last several hours.

A more formidable storm is the squall line or multi-cell line storm, made up of a long line of storms led by a steady, well-developed gust front, a blast of cool air created when a storm cloud's cool downdraft hits the ground and spreads outward. A gust front often produces other storms by lifting surrounding warm air and generating new cells. Squall lines can be more than 100 miles (160 km) long. Strong downdrafts, which are experienced on the ground as blasts of cool air, are their signature.

The most feared type of thunderstorm is the supercell, a storm so self-sustaining it can last for hours and

A thunderstorm's drenching rains are a welcome occurrence in farm country—as long as the storm does not also unleash fierce winds, hail, or destructive lightning.

move independently of the wind. Supercells can produce hail more than two inches (5 cm) in diameter and very strong downbursts. But supercells are also characterized by updrafts of 150 miles (240 km) per hour or more, which, encountering winds from different directions as they rise, begin to rotate in a swirl several miles wide called a **mesocyclone**. Mesocyclones are clearly identifiable on **radar** and can breed violent tornadoes.

Supercell thunderstorms can rise to 10 miles (16 km) or more in altitude, which is higher than commercial jetliners fly. Pilots, knowing what kinds of forces are on the loose in supercells, fly around these dangerous storms. The central U.S. and eastern Australia experience supercells more frequently than any other parts of the world.

In a storm system called a **mesoscale convective complex**, single cells or groups of cells heading from

Many cities in tropical climates are well acquainted with thunderstorms; the coastal city of Miami, Florida (pictured below) sees around 80 such storms every year.

THE RIGHT SPARE CHANGE

*Trained weather spotters in the U.S. often carry a lot of sophisticated gear: Citizens' Band (CB) radios, **barometers**, wind-speed measuring devices, and maybe a computer for tracking radar and other Internet communications. They also carry at least 41 cents. That's the total value of one of each of the four most common U.S. coins—a penny, a nickel, a dime, and a quarter—which are the most common measurements for hail. Weather officials believe people understand the sizes of coins better than fractions of inches or centimeters. Bigger hail is rare, so weather watchers generally do not carry fruit or golf balls.*

the Rocky Mountains toward the American Midwest often merge into large systems. These systems can frequently produce storms lasting six hours or more and bring much-needed rain to the corn- and wheat-growing areas of the central U.S.

People in the western U.S. and Canada often experience a frustrating phenomenon known as a "dry" thunderstorm. Thunderstorms enter the region from the west with plenty of moisture and announce their arrival with impressive displays of lightning and rumbles of thunder, but they frequently pass without dropping any rain. This is because the air beneath them is so dry that falling moisture evaporates before it hits the ground. Without rain to accompany it, lightning from these storms often touches off wildfires. More than 1,000 fires started this way raged across California in June 2008, destroying homes and forests.

Thunderstorms can also generate extremely strong straight-line winds, which push out from downdrafts slamming to the ground. These winds don't normally command the attention tornadoes do, but they can be every bit as dangerous, producing tornado-scale damage. Gust fronts, sometimes with winds moving at up to 100 miles (160 km) per hour, can smash buildings and topple trees. Similar to a gust front is a microburst, a circular downburst with a radius of

Gust fronts, which occur more frequently on the eastern side of North America than the western, are often immediately preceded by a change in wind direction.

less than 2.5 miles (4 km). Circular downbursts that extend more than 2.5 miles (4 km) from the center are called macrobursts.

The biggest bully among downdrafts is the derecho. *Derecho* is a Spanish word meaning "straight," which describes precisely how its winds are different from those of a tornado (a word that also has a Spanish root, *tornar*, meaning "to turn"). Derechos are wide bands of winds associated with squall line thunderstorms, often dozens of miles wide and arranged in a "bow" shape. They plow paths of damage that are often at least 200 miles (322 km) long, sending forth winds that can be 100 miles (160 km) per hour or faster. The entire band of winds commonly moves at about 50 miles (80 km) per hour and can catch people by surprise, even if those people are outside with an eye on the sky.

A derecho on July 4 and 5, 1980, which began near Omaha, Nebraska, and ran more than 1,000 miles (1,600 km) east to the Atlantic Ocean, killed 6 people and injured 67. Four of those killed were in boats. Twenty people were injured in mobile homes that were knocked over, and 19 were hurt by falling trees.

On the same date 19 years later, a derecho that blew up in North Dakota traveled 1,300 miles (2,092 km) eastward across North America before dying over Maine. One of the northernmost derechos on record, it generated winds of 58 to 91 miles (93–146 km) per hour for 39 minutes at Fargo, North Dakota. It then toppled millions of trees in the forests of northern Minnesota and southern Ontario and Quebec. In the Boundary Waters Canoe Area Wilderness of northern Minnesota, trees in an area 12 miles (19 km) wide by 30 miles (48 km) long were completely flattened. In the derecho's path across the continent, 2 people were killed and 70 were injured, almost all of them campers who'd been in the woods or on the water during that hot and muggy Fourth of July weekend.

After seeing the Minnesota damage from that 1999 derecho, U.S. Forest Service ranger Bruce Slover said, "This must be what it looked like in 1910 or 1920, at the end of the logging days." Yet it all happened in a few hours, a testament to the power of thunderstorms.

Although not usually as intense or ferocious as tornadoes, derechos can be even more disruptive to forests and other natural environments due to their wide paths.

"THIS IS THE NATIONAL WEATHER SERVICE ..."

When the automated voice of the National Weather Service issues a severe thunderstorm warning, conditions aren't just going to get loud and wet. They could get dangerous. First, a severe thunderstorm warning suggests the possibility of a tornado, which can form so suddenly there might not be enough time to issue a separate tornado warning. It also means that damaging hail and winds could be on their way. A flash flood might be another consequence. Severe thunderstorm warnings are usually issued for one hour, although they can be refreshed. Environment Canada, that country's climate and weather service, has different standards for its warnings from region to region.

HAIL AND HIGH WATER

It didn't take long for early humans to experience the overpowering effects of a thunderstorm. Only seven chapters into the Bible, shortly after the creation of Heaven and Earth, God sends a storm to wipe out humankind. Only a man named Noah, his family, and a parade of animals survive.

Lightning, thunder, hail, and rain make frequent appearances in the Bible, sometimes representing God or His voice, often as game-changers on the battlefield. Throughout literature, the thunderstorm frequently pushes people to their critical moment, creating terror and confusion and leading them to discover their strengths and vulnerabilities. That's what happens in reality, too.

Late in the spring of 1889, heavy rains fell in Pennsylvania's Conemaugh Valley. On May 30 and 31, eight inches (20 cm) or more from intense storms pushed a lake through a poorly maintained dam on the Little Conemaugh River, triggering the most devastating flash flood in U.S. history. Rampaging through a narrow valley, the water hit the town of Mineral Point, leaving behind nothing but bare rock. In about an hour, a wall of water and debris up to 60 feet (18 m) high and moving at 40 miles (64 km) per hour slammed into the city of Johnstown, home to some 30,000 residents. The flood killed 2,209

people, including as many as 300 who, trapped in a pile of debris that had been jammed against a railroad bridge, died horrible deaths when it caught fire. The calamity prompted the first peacetime relief effort by the American Red Cross.

Although people mostly look up to watch for danger when a thunderstorm approaches, one of the greatest threats can come at ground level in the form of a flash flood.

Thunderstorms that stall over steep-walled valleys like the Little Conemaugh River's have frequently spawned tragic flash floods. On June 9, 1972, warm, moist air running up the eastern side of the Black Hills in South Dakota pushed cumulus clouds high into the sky. Because upper winds were light, they barely moved. That night, more than 12 inches (30 cm) of rain fell in some areas upslope of Rapid City, where about 45,000 people lived.

Within minutes, close to midnight, the volume of water in Rapid Creek swelled to seven times what it had been an hour before and four times the previous record. The water crashed through the city, killing 238 people and doing $164 million in damages. Among those killed were 14 responders from state, local, and federal governments. "It was a night of absolute terror," said Rapid City mayor Don Barnett.

A remarkably similar event took place southwest of the Black Hills four years later, on July 31, 1976. Several thousand people were hiking, camping, and fishing in the Big Thompson River canyon just west of Denver, Colorado, when a wall of cumulus clouds formed over

the Front Range of the Rocky Mountains and stalled. Eight inches (20 cm) of rain fell over the steep canyon, running directly into the Big Thompson River. Soon a mass of water carrying huge boulders tumbled through the canyon, and within 2 hours, 139 people were dead.

While severe thunderstorms take human life, they can also leave huge repair bills. Two weeks of rain in July 1996 led to flash flooding that killed 10 people and forced 16,000 out of their homes in Saguenay, Quebec. It was Canada's most expensive natural disaster ever, with damages approaching $1 billion. A thunderstorm over Dallas, Texas, on May 5, 1995, was the first $1 billion thunderstorm in U.S. history. Tornadoes, flash floods, heavy rains, winds of up to 70 miles (112 km) per hour, and softball-sized hail combined to kill 16 people. An industrial plant collapsed, and thousands of vehicles and homes were damaged.

When heavy rain is channeled into canyons in mountainous terrain, it can result in disaster, as was illustrated by the Big Thompson River flash flood of 1976 (opposite).

LIGHT INTO GLASS

When lightning strikes, it can drill into soils and rocks and melt minerals. When the molten material cools, it forms a glassy, often crazily branched type of hollow stone called a fulgurite, 1 or 2 inches (2.5–5 cm) in diameter but perhaps 10 feet (3 m) or more in length. The term is based on the Latin word for lightning, fulgur. Fulgurites made in sand are usually the longest. (When lightning strikes a rock, it often leaves a fulgurite coating the outside.) Fulgurites are found all over the world, most commonly in Florida, but are relatively rare.

Hail is often overshadowed by tornadoes, straight-line winds, and flooding among a thunderstorm's destructive forces. But hail can cause millions of dollars in damage to homes and vehicles, and it can ruin farmers' crops in mere minutes, as history has frequently shown. A storm over London, England, in 1879 dropped hailstones "as big as teacups," according to one historical account. Falling at 100 miles (160 km) per hour, hailstones that size can drill inches into the ground, strip bark and leaves off trees, and heavily damage buildings. A hailstorm over a car dealership can shatter every windshield and dent each vehicle so extensively that the entire inventory might be a total loss. Hail can certainly injure people, though deaths are rare.

Born in the tops of cumulus clouds (opposite), hail is one of the great weather oddities, falling on some of the hottest days of the year amid summer's green foliage.

Hail is formed when small bits of ice in the top of a cumulus cloud get heavy and fall into a warmer level, where they get coated by water, then are blown up again by the updrafts, where the new coating freezes. Strong updrafts can keep this yo-yo process going for hours sometimes, layering the hailstone with more and more ice until its weight finally overcomes the force of the updraft, and it falls to Earth.

A hailstorm that swept across the southern Midwest on April 10, 2001, ranks as the costliest ever, in part because it pelted the cities of Kansas City, St. Louis,

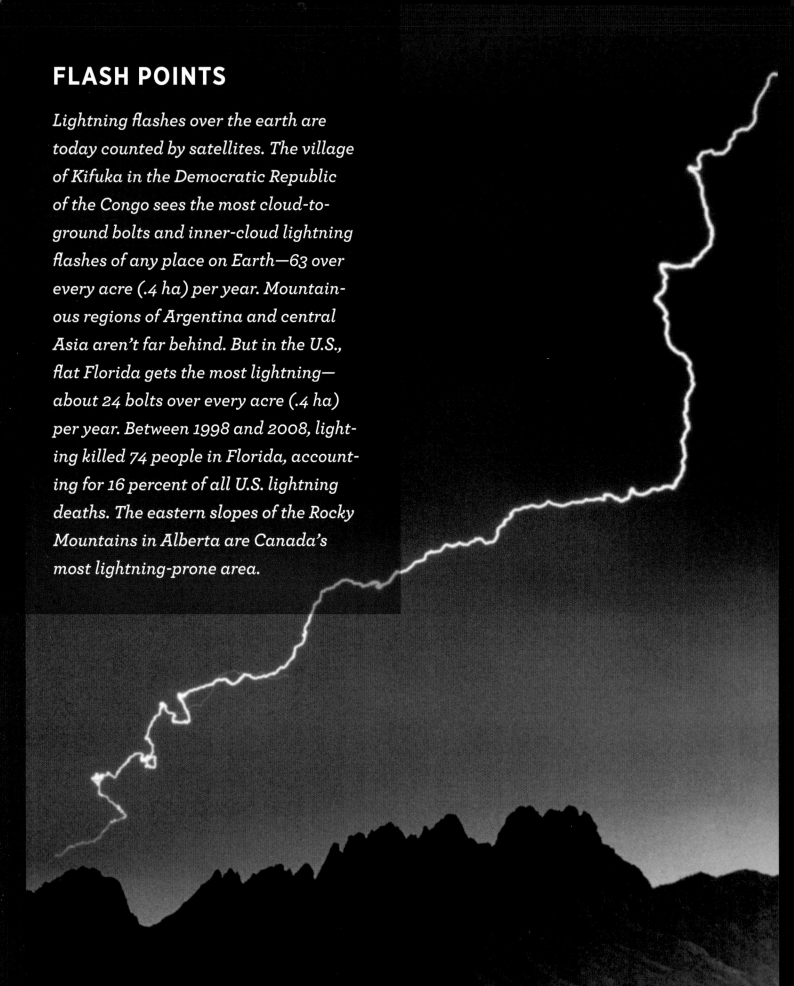

FLASH POINTS

Lightning flashes over the earth are today counted by satellites. The village of Kifuka in the Democratic Republic of the Congo sees the most cloud-to-ground bolts and inner-cloud lightning flashes of any place on Earth—63 over every acre (.4 ha) per year. Mountainous regions of Argentina and central Asia aren't far behind. But in the U.S., flat Florida gets the most lightning—about 24 bolts over every acre (.4 ha) per year. Between 1998 and 2008, lighting killed 74 people in Florida, accounting for 16 percent of all U.S. lightning deaths. The eastern slopes of the Rocky Mountains in Alberta are Canada's most lightning-prone area.

and Columbia, Missouri—heavily built-up areas where insurance claims for damaged buildings and vehicles would naturally be high. The hail ranged from one to three inches (2.5–7.5 cm) in diameter. It damaged every home in Florissant, Missouri, a suburb of St. Louis with about 50,000 residents. The so-called "Tri-State Hailstorm" was also notable simply for its size. The hail fell continuously for 8 hours along a 365-mile (587 km) path from Kansas through Missouri and into Illinois, which is extraordinary because hailstorms are usually brief and local. Although the width of its path—6 to 15 miles (9.6–24 km)—was not unusual, it was the longest hailstorm ever recorded.

The Tri-State Hailstorm was the costliest storm of its kind, even after damages from earlier historic incidents were adjusted for the changing value of the dollar. The damage price tag was $1.5 billion. For the period 1949 through 2001, it was the ninth-costliest weather catastrophe in the U.S.—right behind eight hurricanes. North of America, hailstorms in Calgary, Alberta, on September 7, 1991, and July 24, 1996, each caused more than $300 million in damage and were among the costliest storms in Canadian history.

Global warming research suggests that more—and more intense—thunderstorms might be a feature of an altered climate. But a growing population is itself likely to lead to an increased impact from severe thunderstorms, as more people find themselves caught in the midst of these ferocious acts of nature.

This supercell thunderstorm produced three tornadoes and softball-sized hail; fortunately, since it blew over sparsely populated North Dakota, it did relatively little damage.

THE GREATEST SHOW ABOVE EARTH

Thrilling and frightening, lightning has always been the spectacle most people associate with thunderstorms. Ages ago, it was regarded as the chief weapon of the gods in many cultures. It was also seen as a blessing when it brought early humans the civilizing gift of fire.

In 1752, American statesman and inventor Benjamin Franklin proved by flying his kite in a thunderstorm (a dangerous experiment best left to experts) that lightning was made of electricity. But researchers have learned a lot more about it since then. There are two primary types of lightning: lightning that strikes the earth and lightning that stays within a thundercloud. Some lightning also travels from one cloud to another. Only one of every five lightning bolts leaves the clouds to strike the ground.

Lightning follows a path of air molecules that have been ripped apart, or **ionized**, in rising cumulonimbus clouds. Water and ice being hurled around by updrafts and downdrafts in a cloud will strip **electrons** from each other's molecules. For reasons that still aren't clear, positively charged particles will collect near the top of the cloud, and negatively charged particles will assemble near the bottom. Those charges attract each other, and when the attraction is strong enough, a powerful spark is ignited: a bolt of lightning. Each flash carries the equivalent of 250 kilowatt hours of power, enough to operate a 100-watt light bulb for three months or to run 8,000 toasters at once.

Meanwhile, the thundercloud might also create a "shadow" of positively charged particles along the ground. When the negative charge at the bottom of the cloud and the positive charge on the ground reach a certain strength, they touch off a cloud-to-ground lightning bolt, perhaps half an inch (1.25 cm) wide but a zigzagging five miles (8 km) long. The final segment of a cloud-to-ground lightning bolt actually forms from the ground up. Fifteen million to 20 million of them strike U.S. ground in a year, with another 4 million zapping Canada.

Long before the discoveries of Benjamin Franklin, Norsemen (Scandinavian people commonly known as Vikings) interpreted lightning as the hammer strokes of a god named Thor.

People outdoors are particularly vulnerable to lightning. Of those killed by lightning, about 80 percent are men, probably because, statistically, men are more likely than women to be playing golf or fishing or working in lightning-prone, open areas. Some would say men are more likely too than women to ignore severe weather warnings.

Worldwide, about 40 lightning bolts are striking the earth at any given second, according to the National Atmospheric and Space Administration. Given that fact, it's surprising people don't get hit by it more often than they do. In the U.S., lightning kills more than 60 people per year, making it, on average, the second-most frequent storm-related killer, behind only flooding. Most cloud-to-ground strikes in the U.S. are in the Southeast, with most of the deaths occurring in Florida. In Canada, more than six people are killed by lightning annually.

Although thousands of people are known to get struck by lightning, many incidents never get reported. Victims often don't remember details because they get thrown and knocked unconscious. For some, the shock stops their heartbeat. Some report waking up temporarily paralyzed, with tremendous headaches, or

with buzzing feelings in their teeth, or even with tooth fillings melted. Some smell their own burned flesh. Many find some of their clothes blown apart, zippers fused together, or shoes melted.

"It felt like a car accident, only it happened a thousand times faster," said Kenneth Pickering, who was struck by lightning on a Toronto golf course in 2008, thrown about 15 feet (4.5 m), and knocked unconscious. "It's like I got beat up by a gang with baseball bats. I felt very dizzy, and my feet were so tender that I didn't think I'd be able to walk. My legs were bruised all the way down and my feet were just tingling."

It's estimated that 9 out of 10 people struck by lightning survive. After their initial injuries, they often face long-term problems such as hearing loss, paralysis, and other neurological difficulties. Many also suffer from depression, memory loss, and other psychological problems.

Lightning has its good qualities. It can light up a stormy sky at night, often allowing storm spotters to see funnel clouds and issue tornado warnings. It can also alter nitrogen in the air so that it can be carried by rain into the soil to fertilize plants.

Lightning can be a threat on multiple levels; not only does it send people caught outdoors running for shelter (opposite), but it can trigger hugely destructive wildfires (above).

But like hail, lightning is better known for its destructive power. Lightning can knock out power stations and transformers, interrupting electrical power to thousands of homes at a time. It can split trees, set homes on fire, and, upon entering homes through the wiring, has been known to kill people as they talk on landline telephones. It can destroy computers and other electrical appliances and give occupants a jolt if they reach for a faucet handle or anything attached to metal plumbing, which it also uses to invade a house.

Pilots try to fly around thunderstorms, but most U.S. commercial planes take at least one lightning hit per year. The plane's aluminum skin is able to pass the charge to tips on the plane's wings or tail and back out to the air, so the passengers don't feel any shock. A plane crash has not been attributed to a lightning strike since a fuel tank explosion caused a plane to go down in Maryland in 1963, killing 81 people. That incident represents one of the greatest number of deaths known from a single lightning incident. Fuel tanks on planes now have extra protection against lightning and sparks.

Most fatal lightning strikes claim one or two victims and hardly even become news. But lightning is always dangerous. Lightning can strike "out of the blue"—as far as six miles (10 km) from a thundercloud. Generally,

CLUNK!

A hailstone that fell in Aurora, Nebraska, on June 22, 2003, holds the official distinction as the largest ever recovered in the U.S. It measured 7 inches (18 cm) in diameter and nearly 19 inches (48 cm) in circumference, even though it had broken after crashing into the roof of a home. However, it was irregularly shaped, raising some questions as to how best to measure hailstones, since few are perfectly round. Some researchers say a hailstone's weight would offer better comparisons. The Aurora hailstone weighed about 1.1 pounds (0.5 kg); another from the same storm was smaller but heavier.

NEW TYPES OF LIGHTNING

Pilots, satellites, and astronauts have documented forms of lightning that flash upward above storm clouds. Faint, red bursts known as sprites can extend upward as far as 60 miles (96 km). Sprites happen simultaneously with lightning below but are produced by fewer than 1 in 100 lightning flashes. Rarer still are blue jets—vivid, cone-shaped flashes from the cloud tops to an altitude of about 25 miles (40 km). Scientists believe sprites and blue jets may balance electrical charges throughout Earth's atmosphere. They occasionally can be seen atop storm clouds from a distance of more than 100 miles (160 km).

the safest places to be when lightning is in the area are indoors—away from windows or outer walls—or in a vehicle with all the doors and windows closed. Outside, people should crouch down or get in a low spot and away from isolated trees, flagpoles, or other tall objects. Lightning can strike anywhere, but it often is electrically attracted to tall, exposed structures.

Because more than 50 percent of all lightning-caused deaths happen after the thunderstorm has passed, it's wise to wait 30 minutes after hearing the last of the thunder before heading outside. By then, the sun may have etched a rainbow across the dark clouds of the retreating storm—a sort of colorful peace offering after a thunderstorm's awesome violence.

From the rumble of a storm cloud to the spectacular colors of a rainbow, a summer thunderstorm can be a weather event of unparalleled sights and sounds.

GLOSSARY

ANVIL, n. — *an iron or steel tool against which to hammer and shape metal; it is wide and flat on top of a smaller base*

AQUIFERS, n. — *pockets of water deep below ground, often tapped for drinking water and crop irrigation*

BAROMETERS, n. — *devices that measure atmospheric pressure, usually using a metallic element called mercury that moves up or down in a tube*

CIRCUMFERENCE, n. — *the distance around an object or shape*

CONDENSE, v. — *to form a liquid from a vapor*

CONVECTIVE, adj. — *describing the vertical movement of heat and moisture*

CUMULUS, adj. — *describing a low-level cloud resembling cauliflower, which typically forms in summer and often swells into a storm producer*

CURRENT, n. — *in electricity, a flow of electrical charges*

DECIBELS, n. — *levels of loudness ranked from 0 (the softest sounds) to 160 (a jet takeoff at close range), the loudest of which can do instant and permanent ear damage*

DIAMETER, n. — *the widest distance across a circle or through a ball*

DISSIPATING, v. — *weakening and then scattering or vanishing*

ELECTRONS, n. — *negatively charged particles within atoms; atoms are basic units of nature that cannot be broken down into smaller units*

EVAPORATE, v. — *to turn from a liquid into a vapor*

INFRASONIC, adj. — *describing a pitch of sound too low for humans to hear*

IONIZED, adj. — *describing a molecule that has had one or more electrons added or removed*

MESOCYCLONE, n. — *a rotating area of a thunderstorm, two to six miles (3–10 km) in diameter and about five miles (8 km) above the ground, in which tornadoes often form*

MESOSCALE, adj. — *in meteorology, ranging in coverage area from about 50 to 100 miles (80–160 km) across*

RADAR, n. — *a system that uses radio waves bounced off objects, such as planes or raindrops, to determine their location, size, and speed; the word stands for Radio Detecting and Ranging*

STRATOSPHERE, n. — *the second level of Earth's atmosphere, extending from about 10 to 30 miles (16–50 km) up, just beyond the troposphere*

SUPERCELL, n. — *part of a system of thunderstorms that develops in such a way that it can continue to feed itself on updrafts of warm, moist air*

SUPERSONIC, adj. — *traveling faster than the speed of sound*

Douglas, Paul. *Restless Skies: The Ultimate Weather Book.* New York: Sterling, 2005.

Kahl, Jonathan D. W. *National Audubon Society First Field Guide: Weather.* New York: Scholastic, 1998.

Murphree, Tom, and Mary K. Miller. *Watching Weather.* New York: Henry Holt, 1998.

National Lightning Safety Institute. "Lightning Incidents." http://www.lightningsafety.com/nlsi_lls .html.

National Severe Storms Laboratory. Severe Weather Primer: "Thunderstorm Basics." National Oceanic and Atmospheric Administration. http:// www.nssl.noaa.gov/primer/tstorm/tst_basics.html.

Storm Prediction Center. "About Derechos." National Oceanic and Atmospheric Administration /National Weather Service. http://www.spc.noaa .gov/misc/AbtDerechos/derechofacts.htm.

USA Today. "Resources: Thunderstorms." USAToday.com. http://www.usatoday.com/weather/ resources/basics/thunderstorms.htm.

Watts, Alan. *The Weather Handbook.* 2nd ed. Dobbs Ferry, N.Y.: Sheridan House, 1999.

INDEX